The Translator's Diary

Jon Pineda

New Issues Poetry & Prose

A Green Rose Book

New Issues Poetry & Prose
The College of Arts and Sciences
Western Michigan University
Kalamazoo, Michigan 49008

First Edition, 2008.

ISBN-10   1-930974-75-2 (paperbound)
ISBN-13   978-1-930974-75-3 (paperbound)

Library of Congress Cataloging-in-Publication Data:
Pineda, Jon
The Translator's Diary/Jon Pineda
Library of Congress Control Number: 2007939096

Editor   William Olsen
Managing Editor   Marianne Swierenga
Copy Editor   Natalie Giarratano
Designer   Breana Robinson
Art Director   Tricia Hennessy
Production Manager   Paul Sizer
                                The Design Center, Frostic School of Art
                                College of Fine Arts
                                Western Michigan University
Printing   Cushing-Malloy, Inc.

The Translator's Diary

Jon Pineda

For Anne,

So great to see you again! Many thanks & take care,

Jon

Queens MFA '09

New Issues

WESTERN MICHIGAN UNIVERSITY

Also by Jon Pineda

Birthmark

for Amy

There beside him she stood,—
And he, perplexed;

—Theodore Roethke

Contents

Coma

What if I told you
each time you whispered
my name it felt like a door
I could place a hand against,
feel how warm it was, as if
the world on the other side,
yours, was the one on fire?

I.

And breathed upon it till at last it burned
Uncertainly, among the stars its sisters—
Breathe on me still, star, sister.
                              —Randall Jarrell

First Snowfall

Snow layered itself
over the already dead,

those clumps of tomato
plants I'd neglected

from the summer
crumpled under drifts,

their bones muscled
with cold near the shed.

I spoke your name,
and it spun there,

our little ghost,
spreading open

its arms until they
were bare limbs

of trees, my neighbor's
broken fence, this

bright distance
between us.

Visiting Hours

A pattern of stars
pressed on the wind-
shields of cars below.

Days we spend in shifts,
gaze out the window
onto drifts of snow.

As streets fill with plows
plying back the cold layer,
the city aglow in its coma,

we watch from the room
the world's slow thaw
like your heart forever

threatening to bloom.

Losing A Memory

After watching a woman's fingers sink into bread
        and scatter its pieces over a river,

I have tried to remember how water held part
of an evening sun, itself held back by a shadow of spires

on the hill, gently tapping along the Vltava until
swans disrupted the water.

        It was almost communion,

and yet this thought of almost being *something* slowly passed
as the swans bundled together, diving one after the other.

Earlier, I thought I saw her in the crowd
rising out of the metro stop at Staromestska,

her eyes opening the way each umbrella spread
        with rain ending in the street.

It was only the way those strangers disappeared,
huddled and turning into alleyways, sound.

        A horn made me realize

I was standing too close to the curb.
The driver screamed in his language as he passed,

shaking his fist into a subsiding fury.
I have forgotten or remembered.

Whenever I think of death, her absence becomes a sheath
of wings disappearing into a dark body, or a candlewick

giving into its own weight and slipping beneath a surface
that will harden, maybe to be relit tomorrow night,

adding its light to the shadowy room of a café
where a woman reads aloud from a book she has written,

                poem after poem,

about love.

The Statue

Searching the city
for the statue, we
found it expressionless
in a cathedral, a child
holding the world
out to anyone.

We had no money.
We drank thin soup
for lunch. Gypsies laughed
at tourists, while in bars
skinheads peered at other
tables and did not speak.

It was how it was.

Walking through Old Town
Square, we saw a man piss
his name on cobblestones,
harsh consonants vanished
among the vowels.

He stumbled, steadied
himself against a wall.
Neither one of us said,
Are you all right?
Some things are
never misunderstood.

On Charles Bridge,
statues of saints left
shadows over a circle
of those playing guitars.
A girl stood up and
swayed in its radius.

We froze as she held
out her hands, palms

open as if she might
catch the stars
raining down
on us all.

Blackbird

Luke, at two years old, takes his mother's open hand
and tells us that she's holding a *blackbird*, her palm
curved, it seems, under the weight. It makes us smile.

Later, after you've fallen asleep, I find your hand
under covers, run my finger inside the warm
cusp and touch, for the first time, its wings.

Brunelleschi

Since the tendency of the masonry
is to fold from within, there were designs
put in place, like metaphors, for building
the dome; its herringbone pattern
of brickwork leveled the circular skeleton
rounding the frame in nine diminishing
rings all raising skyward, an echo
from the flamed circles of Dante's *Inferno* born
somewhere below the sprawl of Florence.
I see you in this same way, before
the dome rose, when there was always
a fear of one raised so high on scaffolding,
even their looking down into the chasm
would prompt them to lean inward.

My Sister, Who Died Young, Takes Up The Task

A basket of apples brown in our kitchen,
their warm scent is the scent of ripening,

and my sister, entering the room quietly,
takes a seat at the table, takes up the task

of peeling slowly away the blemished skins,
even half-rotten ones are salvaged carefully.

She makes sure to carve out the mealy flesh.
For this, I am grateful. I explain, *this elegy*

would love to save everything. She smiles at me,
and before long, the empty bowl she uses fills,

domed with thin slices she brushes into
the mouth of a steaming pot on the stove.

What can I do? I ask finally. *Nothing,*
she says, *let me finish this one thing alone.*

Cinque Terre

Between the train's long slide and the sun
ricocheting off the sea, anyone
would have fallen silent in those words,
the language of age in her face, the birds
cawing over the broken earth, gathering near its stones
and chapel doors. In the marina, the sea and its bones
have grown smaller. Though the tide is out,
it is not the tide nor the feathers nor the cat
that jumps into the street, the dust
lifting with each wing and disappearing. The rust-
colored sheets that wrap the sails of ships,
I don't know their name nor the way to say *lips
of water* in Italian and mean this: an old woman
stood by the tracks until his hand stopped waving.

Reflection

Morning light gathers in the river.
The blue heron with its wings spread wide
between the many worlds of its reflection.

A couple sits on a bench and listens to their
son, newborn, whispering what can only be
the last of some message brought with him.

The great bird pauses among clouds and cool air.
Beside the small library yet to open, the wife points
to houses on the other side where they could see
themselves living at some point in their lives.

There would be more children, perhaps even
a dog bounding about the backyard fenced
with tufts of cord grass, the Elizabeth still
touching this edge of the dream as well.

When a door opens behind them, the tall
librarian waves from a distance. They don't
realize this man is only shielding his eyes
from the sun. It changes nothing at all.

The Conversation

Take the time
my brother, just a boy,
sat alone in the house
and spoke to the stray.
Nestled in a blanket
faded as the ocean is
some days, the cat lay
swollen with trinkets.
Intent, my brother stroked
a streak of hair under
the cat's throat, curlicued
with fluid, as one by one
its young slid out in glazed
wrapping, each cradling
a purse of blood and blue
meat, all of it a kind of food
the mother struggled to eat.

Departure

Near the bent awning
of the station, a bird
built its nest with strands
of ribbon and bandages.
In the implication,
you found yourself
held briefly as the train
began its departure
through those faces
blurring until they were
nothing but green stalks,
a pasture of wildflowers
yet to be woven.

II.

And then a Plank in Reason, broke
And I dropped down, and down—
And hit a World, at every plunge
                    —Emily Dickinson

The Translator's Diary

1.

The ocean was never quite glass.

There were swimmers. Bodies breathing
water. The numerous, luminous things.

An ocean's remains. Shoddy gulls
tore through strings of abandoned fruit

woven in sand near the smeared ashes
of a bonfire. There, and the truth,

how it never survives its translation.

2.

One listens to the unbroken waves.

Within the shadow of the swell,
where shadow falls among its current,

a raft with a girl lounging in this fallen
light of day sways in the straying path.

What is minute is broken, bright
triangles of glass break and form.

For now, the girl lost, dreaming.
Her friends listen to a radio wedged in sand.

There is only the talk of weather. Ice-
cold bottles. Then songs. Today is nothing

but blue skies.

3.

Where the tireless sand is at work,
the walls of a turret near collapse.

Children run along the shoreline,
dive in and become their shadows.

One watches the struggle
to become this moment.

A brief silence folds within
each crawl then kicks. Their skin.

What listens to itself breathing.
What is lulled by the breath's cadence.

The further down they go,
the more they will know the darkness.

A soft life once held within each shell
left this life for the next one.

Various shells break open, spill
themselves across the shoreline,

and join the churn of breaking each
path along the beach reaches.

Scattering light. The light scattering
of shells on blankets. From umbrella creases,

the voices of children vanish into
the voices of parents calling for them.

4.

        From crests
to troughs, a squadron of pelicans.

And there is the lone *something*
with the fate of the world on its back.

Before the sun goes down, one listens
to a gull circle into its one complaint.

What is spoken will go unsaid again.
A couple walks a good length of the beach.

They are washed in light briefly, nearly
feel themselves slide into silhouettes

where they find a leg of driftwood, still damp,
and in one of the grooves, a butterfly caught,

its own leg clamped in a soft fold of bark.
The slow-beating wings join their breathing.

5.

Then the wind that begins with the butterfly.
The carefully-patted air that becomes a storm.

Where the current takes another form,
the ocean is forever an implication.

A shell lifted to the ear. A name
that is only its echo accelerating

into the calm of the beach, where
a couple reappears over the next dune.

Sand anchored by roots of sea oats.
The wind stirs the dune's face loose.

6.

Within a quiet thicket of skulls,
hollow sandspurs wait to attach.

Red lines rise alongside her ankle.
He takes her foot into his hands.

Brushing away the sand, murmuring,
he places his lips over each place.

Into the quiet again. Into light colliding
on cars lining the unnamed boulevard.

Rows of cottages' windows blink on and off
before the void of the ocean finds them.

What is whole is momentary, breaks
apart into a swaying fence of oats,

into paths that disappear.

7.

Where there is a truck filled with sand,
there is a car filled with teenagers.

Where there is a sign fading in the sun,
there is a girl's bare foot slipping from the brake

and the wide-eyed look of the driver
before trying to swerve the truck still sliding.

The way light drapes on a windshield.

One of the girls in the car wakes then
from her dream of floating on a raft.

She finds the waves have moved inland,
spilling over the road and filling the car.

Where glass becomes pieces of ocean,
the void carries them away.

8.

Among the quiet of a room, one
speaks forever with her hands.

She fashions birds with broken wings,
releases them onto the floor to scurry.

Like the story of the killdeer.
How it pretends its wing is hurt, unfolded,

to lure the one hovering away from its nest.
This is a sacrifice for the sake of the brood.

In one moment, the girl eases into the ocean.
In another moment, the girl never walks again.

Busily rendering, the image always
temporal and yet always

9.

a little life inside the papery cell.
Another life inside the coma.

There, in a window you waited
all spring to open, a filled nest

where hornets fell onto the sill,
their armor like ancient warriors

with eyes the color of clay.
An emperor's army dormant in the earth,

while in the garden, her hands once
unearthed bulbs of jonquils and irises,

shells of hornets. The wet smell
of fresh graves.

10.

But again, quietly, like snowfall
on the TV, news of an earthquake from

the other side of the world.
Within the basilica, frescoes slid

from walls and tumbled into shards.

When the effort to rebuild begins
with those sifting through the clutter,

in chaos, each color will form on its own
in the hoarding of fragments, rough

or smooth, carefully pieced together
until, moment by moment, the image emerges.

11.

And if the couple appearing on the dune
becomes, instead, a brother and a sister

holding hands while the sand whips
around their legs in small funnels,

they will not be carried away.
Not yet. There

will still be a door
the boy must open onto the ICU

and find his sister, who is older,
lying in bed with half

of her head shaved, the thick
black hair vanished

into a night full of stars.
The memory will stay with him,

like his first real kiss,
like the sharp scent of cut apples

12.

before turning. Stay with him.
The boy wants nothing more

than to believe a girl he knew
in high school never sat alone

in a room with a gun.
That same year, reading the *Inferno*

and passages on the Suicides,
their branches breaking endlessly,

he thinks of the girl's grief
as only a dress leaving the body

for the back of a chair, the fabric
translucent it is so thin, a breath

of red, and how care could have been
taken to ease the cloth, folding it so,

the memory of her legs erased
into a room where blinds turned

blocking the sun.

13.

Stay with him. It will be years
before he considers the girl again. Alone,

markers like stone crop in the blond grass,
visiting the grave of his sister,

he finds only a few feet away
the girl he knew in high school

and crouches in the field, head bowed
like a gardener intent on pulling weeds,

feels along the dirt before reaching
the cold letters of her name.

What is it then for him to say
another's name and watch it become

a globe of breath before a field,
where the land resembles more a frozen lake

than the vast, marbled grass of autumn?

14.

And there, in the distance,
broken stalks, corn softening

from the fallen rain, where a gray
fence of distance falls like a curtain

over the stones in a field, a farm
nearby and so close, one riderless horse

pauses from its ritual of pacing
the perimeter and leans its throat

against the barbed wire in hopes
of reaching one tuft still filled

with color, calling its name.

15.

Or, simply, the story. Before the image,
there is the story before the image.

Recorded in footprints on sand,
then sand swept clean by wings

dragged in circles along the ground.
The spiraling. Or the horse amazed

by its luck to find among its life
some trace of summer

when there, briefly, was one

who never woke from the dream
but dipped, instead, her arm into

the ocean, a coma, enough
to feel whole forever.

III.

How should I finish my fragment?
—Boris Pasternak

Cleared Fields

Herefords rummage
cleared fields of cotton.

Here the trodden rows
form an absence of birds.

A hawk above it all pauses
on the invisible cog and spins.

There is no turning back.
There never was.

Broken Images

1.

We glimpse
what nothing must feel like,
a reflection on water, thin,
delicate as your wrist dipping
into the calm river where
the danger in any moment
eddies about, swirling. Consider
the nest of cottonmouths,
the ghost of it so visible on air,
the story goes like this:

a girl had fallen waterskiing,
and when her friends circled
around to find her, someone said
they hung from her
like little black necklaces,
and when this startles you
awake, you find evening
has settled in, slipped its way
through sycamores along
the lush banks, and this alone,
the ease at which darkness returns,
finds its place in this world,
scares you more than anything.

2.

Driving home one night through North Carolina,
on a back road that passed near our mother's
family's farm, the smell of sharp mud in the air,
we could barely see the road before us, even
with the brights on and the way light swayed out.
Before it happened, I remember we laughed
about something I'm sure neither one of us could
recall now, even if someone were to place a gun to
our head, pushing us, trying to scare the hell out of us,
I'll bet we wouldn't remember what made us stop
watching the road, even though it was difficult to
see anything in front of us, anything at all, so hard
to make out even the bright yellow lines glaring
now, this is when the doe lifted into view, softly
placing itself before us as we sped into the night
veering, and the deer must have thought we were nothing
more than a fence it had to cross, because that is
how it came upon us, in midair, and God, I can't
remember what it was that must have made us
laugh out loud beforehand, that caused us to become
distracted in an instant, but one thing I do remember
is the animal's nose, soft and black, reflecting what
I want to think was starlight, and nothing else.

3.

Because we sometimes take each other's stories
for our own, I want to believe I am part of this one,
one where a stray splayed under the crawlspace
of a new building. Tenants were complaining
that all they could hear was a dog whimpering,
the pathetic lilt building like waves from the
ground up until their rooms were filled with it,
nothing but pain, someone said it sounded like,
their small apartments only full of this one sound.
What is amazing is that it went on all day until,
in the story, they call the fire department,
because someone thought it was the right thing
to do, and in comes this rookie, dressed in full
gear while the others, veterans, some who have
spent their lives diving into nothing but black
smoke, pass the time telling each other jokes.
And where I am in this story? I'm laughing,
there on the truck, when the rookie brings back
the dog, heavy, sprawled like a sack of potatoes,
and it doesn't take much to know that it's carrying
a litter, its nipples bright pink like buds on a dogwood.
When he rests her on the ground, he
looks up at us, this kid, this look about him that
says he was prepared for anything, and I love him.

4.

When grief becomes the only thing, you live in broken images—
a girl pulled from the water and covered with snakes,

or the doe who smashes a headlight on a car, and then,
rises like something not of this earth, vanishes into night,

or even fiction, someone else's story you overhear one day
at work, how a firefighter rescued a stray, and in its belly,

you imagine, the utter darkness that rests there, swirling
about in the warm water, waiting its turn to be born.

The Answer

Had it already vanished, been carried
away piece by piece by crows, those
dark angels, I might have been spared.
Instead, it lay beside the road
as if simply out of breath. Gone
onto one side, it spilled its mess
of blue intestines mixed with
smooth stones, the dome of its life
broken within burnt orange fur.
My son, nestled in his car seat,
asked again about the dog he spotted,
and though I searched my mind
for just the right answer, I knew
the day would never come.

Heaven

We brought our children
to the cows at the dairy farm.
In one barn, calves chewed
on strings still holding
together the gate, and beyond,
in the dark pool of a field,
their mothers heavy with milk
raised themselves out of the mud
and roamed the blond grass
in newly-caked boots, their
mouths pruned from saltlick.
Before leaving, we found
a pen filled with ones nearly
grown, their young square ears
pinned with yellow tags, markered
on each were their names, *Heaven*
and *Velvet*, which I read to our son
as he sifted through straws of hay
matted in the dirt, found one
the color of bone and lifted it
nervously to Heaven's
pale tongue.

Messenger

Asleep in the dark
space, a cluster of stars
in the brain, there,

one more dream
before we call her to us
in the hushed room,

and she enters, almost
reverent, our messenger
with head bowed down

in ritual, my hands held
out to catch her, no,
to welcome her home.

The Conversation

She sat, staring up into the light. This had been
her kitchen, everything in sight. Elsewhere, others
talked. One wanted to shave the rest of her head
to match, and so they did, one whispering to her
while the other held clippers, took off remnants
of hair, and she was pleasant, which made it, sad
to say, bearable. They were careful not to touch
the jagged gash. It still seemed fresh, and they were
careful not to stare as hair fell across her shoulders.
The one guiding the clippers felt ashamed for sharing
the moment with them, and the other, who was her
husband, kept touching her face, whispering to her,
while in another room, others talked, and she,
listening, answered only the light.

Song

Because we come from the dream,
I am singing our daughter to sleep.

Shades drawn in our room keep
away what they can, though

there is still the whirring sound
of a plane outside, circling above

before landing at the base nearby.
Newborn, our daughter's heft is barely

there in the cradle of my arms.
I look down and find her fingers

reaching for my voice.
It leaves us both.

Hunters

With light near shadows
grazing the chilled grass,
they walk slowly and in
doing so remove the dark

that follows just behind
them, falls to the ground
until all at once, it seems,
they become father and son,

a man and a boy, and the world
suddenly opens ahead of each
step, air unfolds like a pair
of hands once clasped in prayer

now simply open, welcoming.
Below this sky filled with
broken clouds, the boy recalls
a time when, searching a creek

during lowtide, he'd found
the geode he and his friends
had carried back to the road
and smashed with chunks of

pavement they'd lifted from
the dead end. It broke open.
It spilled its splintery
crystals over the tarmac,

and the boy stopped laughing,
though his friends continued on,
he saw how the stars spread over
the sticky black and knew then

some things in this world
go unnoticed for a reason.
Those friends, he doesn't think
of them when he follows the morning

with his father, and the two,
at different times, glance back
to see their steps have gathered
on the risen dew as the sky

warms, they feel their breathing
heavier underneath coats, their
hearts swelling in the excitement
of knowing deer are blending within

the growing wall of trees. Nearby,
a sound in the brush becomes a flutter
of wings, becomes a random bird that
swirls skyward and fades within

its own song. The two look at
one another. In the son's quick smile,
the father sees traces of himself,
but as someone better, someone else,

and the son, out of the corner
of his eye, sees a doe
and pretends, for a moment,
that he has seen nothing.

Freight

And how it comes to you
in another version, curled
in your arms, your son needing
tonight to fall asleep this way,
rocking him when, almost out,
he is startled by a sound outside
the house. Touching your face,
he whispers, *What was that?*
and you say, because you know
he loves trains, *It was just a train.*
Oh, he answers, three years old
but already so serious, his small face
intent until it finds what you've said
and relaxes. He is drifting again.
This time the weighted train
sounds its horn as it carries
its freight through Norfolk.
What was that? your son says,
though his eyes are barely open,
and continuing on, you softly
shush him as you listen finally
to the filling in of such distance.

Coda

Waking Hours

She wakes in the quiet
house, long shades drawn,
the glass lit with cold.

On the lawn, a fallen snow-
man appears to float in
the blue that glows. Soon

the low sound of a train
returns to the room again,
where there is only this

thought of parting, the
heart pressing syllables
against the dark.

Acknowledgments

Grateful acknowledgment is made to the editors of the following journals, where these poems first appeared, some in slightly different versions:

Blackbird: "First Snowfall" and "Heaven"

Crab Orchard Review: "Cinque Terre," "My Sister, Who Died Young, Takes Up The Task," "Reflection," and "Song"

Drunken Boat: "Coma"

42 Opus: "Visiting Hours"

Hayden's Ferry Review: "Losing A Memory"

Prairie Schooner: "Brunelleschi"

2nd Avenue: "The Statue"

RATTLE: "The Conversation"

Sou'wester: "Broken Images"

The Drunken Boat: "Blackbird" and "Hunters"

Web Del Sol Chapbooks (selected by Bino Realuyo): "Messenger"

"Losing A Memory" also appeared in the anthology *Asian American Poetry: The Next Generation* (University of Illinois Press, 2004), edited by Victoria M. Chang.

"My Sister, Who Died Young, Takes Up The Task" also appeared in the anthology *Contemporary Voices from the Eastern World: An Anthology of Poems* (W.W. Norton, 2008), edited by Tina Chang, Nathalie Handal, and Ravi Shankar.

"Coma," "My Sister, Who Died Young, Takes Up The Task," "The Statue," "Messenger," and "Losing A Memory" are featured in the online audio project *From The Fishouse*, www.fishouse poems.org, edited by Matt O'Donnell.

Many, many thanks to these early readers for their guidance and friendship: Laurie Kutchins, Joseph Legaspi, Nick Montemarano, Oliver de la Paz, and Patrick Rosal.

Kundiman, Kundiman, Kundiman—Sarah Gambito, Josephus Maximus, Oliver de la Paz, Vikas Menon, Jennifer Chang, and our family of poets at www.kundiman.org

To all at New Issues Poetry & Prose, I'm indebted and grateful.

photo by Amy Pineda

Jon Pineda's first collection *Birthmark* was selected by Ralph Burns
as winner of the 2003 Crab Orchard Award Series in Poetry Open
Competition. The recipient of a Virginia Commission for the Arts
Individual Artist Fellowship, he teaches in the English Department
at Old Dominion University and in the MFA program in Creative
Writing at Queens University of Charlotte. He lives in Norfolk,
Virginia, with his wife, Amy, and their two children.

New Issues Poetry